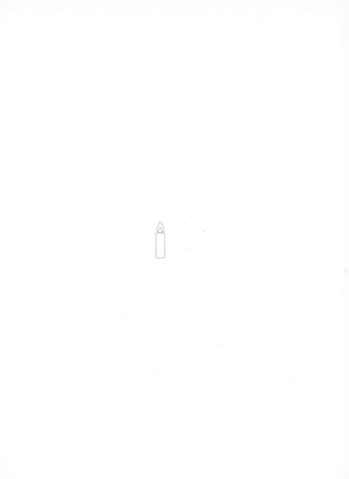

Also available in this series from Quadrille:

the little book of
HOPE

Hardie Grant

QUADRILLE

Hope

Definition:
noun

A feeling of expectation and desire for a particular thing to happen.

verb

To want something to happen or be the case/expect with confidence/ cherish a desire for something to be the case.

"Hope is the only good that is common to all men; those who have nothing else possess hope still."

THALES OF MILETUS

"In the land of hope, there is never any winter."

Russian proverb

"No matter how long the night is, the morning is sure to come."

Congolese proverb

> *"It's good to hope; it's the waiting that spoils it."*

Yiddish proverb

"Hope is the last thing ever lost."

Italian proverb

*"If it were not for Hope,
the heart would break."*

THOMAS FULLER, M.D.

Symbols of hope

Starting life from humble beginnings, the butterfly has long been a symbol of hope. Just as the lowly caterpillar emerges from its cocoon a new, magnificent creature, so, too, will you emerge stronger from your darkest moments.

The candle, with its gentle glow, provides a glimmer of hope in the darkest of times. Enduring, warm and comforting, the flame reminds us that there is a flicker of hope to be found in every situation.

"He [Aristotle] was asked to define hope, and he replied, 'It is a waking dream.'"

DIOGENES

The word 'hope' is an ancient word that probably descends from the Old English *hopian* or the Low Frisian *hopia*. It is perhaps no coincidence that all of these terms contain the word 'hop': when taking the path from darkness to light, a hop or leap of faith may well be needed.

"Hope
Smiles from the threshold of the year to come
Whispering, 'It will be happier'."

ALFRED LORD TENNYSON
The Foresters

Great news for hopeful students!

In 2019, researchers at the University of Qom, Iran, reported in the *Journal of Medical Education Development* that hopeful students are more able to avoid burnout than their peers. They show higher levels of motivation, too.

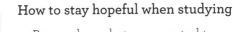

How to stay hopeful when studying

1. Remember what you wanted to achieve when you began. Say, 'I am studying because I hope to. . .'

2. Bring others into your field of hope. Say, 'I hope my studies will allow me to help/inspire. . .'

3. Set aspirations and goals outside of your work so that, even when studying doesn't go to plan, you still have something to look forward to.

Unlike its evil twin, wishful thinking, hope is clear-sighted. Hope responds to facts and possibilities about the likelihood of future events, while wishful thinking does not. Where hope allows for the possibility of a Caribbean holiday after a year of saving up, wishful thinking forgets to plan and is left stranded when the credit card won't work.

Hope always. . .

Smiles

Waits

Guides

Encourages

Supports

Helps

'Hope springs eternal', that most famous epigram about hope, comes from Alexander Pope's 'An Essay on Man', completed in 1731. The great poet attempted to explain God's plans for mankind and says that, though we may not fully understand them, with hope, we can trust that it is all for the best. The poem was warmly received across 18th-century Europe, with Pope's optimistic philosophy gaining popularity among the intelligentsia.

"Hope humbly then; with trembling pinions soar;
Wait the great teacher Death; and God adore!
What future bliss, he gives not thee to know,
But gives that hope to be thy blessing now.
Hope springs eternal in the human breast:
Man never is, but always to be blest:
The soul, uneasy and confin'd from home,
Rests and expatiates in a life to come."

ALEXANDER POPE
'An Essay on Man', Epistle III

Like a warm breeze, hope blows gently
through all of life's momentous events.

Hoping for the right grades...

Hoping the first date goes well...

Hoping she will say yes...

Hoping the pregnancy test
is positive...

Let hope act as a gentle breeze elevating your spirits. Let hope blow away the cold wind of fear that shutters you inside and keeps you away from all that makes life magnificent.

Sometimes, nurturing your hopes and dreams, and, indeed, saying them out loud, can make you feel a little foolish. But do not lose heart. The more you tend to your hopes, the stronger they will burn.

Some of the great philosophers praised the wonders of having a hopeful outlook on life.

In the *Philebus*, Plato records a dialogue between Socrates and Protarchus, in which they discuss the idea that pleasures are essential to a well-lived life. Socrates identifies hope as a pleasure – the 'pleasure of anticipation'. So, if hope is acceptable to Socrates, it ought also to be acceptable to us.

Hope is not. . .

Blind optimism

Wishful thinking

Self-deception

Denial

"We spend our whole lives as full of hope for the future as can be."

SOCRATES

"*The coward, then, is a despairing sort of person; for he fears everything. The brave man, on the other hand, has the opposite disposition; for confidence is the mark of a hopeful disposition.*"

ARISTOTLE

Hope is an entirely forward-looking emotion and action. Imagine hope as a slingshot flinging your dreams into the future and pulling you towards them.

Three reasons to feel hopeful about nature

1. **1 trillion trees will be planted by 2050.** In an unprecedented joint venture between BirdLife International, Wildlife Conservation Society (WCS) and WWF, the Trillion Trees initiative seeks to end deforestation and restore tree cover.

2. **10 animal species no longer in danger of extinction.** The giant panda, southern white rhino, Louisiana black bear, grey wolf, Steller sea lion, American crocodile, grey whale, North Island brown kiwi,

bald eagle and Monito gecko are no longer critically endangered, thanks to the efforts of conservationists and governments, who have helped to protect their wellbeing and restore their habitats.

3. **Beavers roam free in the UK.** After being eradicated from England in the 17th century, beavers have now been reintroduced to the English countryside. Fifteen family groups of beavers now live happily in Devon, busily creating dams and helping to stop flooding.

trilliontrees.org
wwf.org.uk

" *We have always held to the hope, the belief, the conviction, that there is a better life, a better world, beyond the horizon.* "

FRANKLIN D. ROOSEVELT

Three reasons to feel hopeful about humans

1. **Life lasts longer.** In 1870, the life expectancy in Europe, the Americas and the world was 36, 35 and 30 respectively. Today, it is 81, 79 and 72.

2. **The planet's getting greener.** Roughly 40% of the planet has seen 'greening' between 1981 and 2016.

3. **More people can read.** In 1820, only 12 in every 100 people could read; today, it's 85 in every 100.

Be hopeful, for humans have already. . .

Walked on the moon.

Eradicated smallpox.

Domesticated wolves, so we can have puppies.

Discovered electricity.

Produced Prince and 'Purple Rain'.

Evolved the ability to orgasm.

Mapped the human genome.

Invented salted caramel ice cream.

In 1958, SS *Hope* set sail with 100 doctors and 150 nurses on board. The ship belonged to the charity Project HOPE, and she undertook 11 voyages across the globe, from Peru to Tunisia, bringing medical knowledge and improved healthcare systems to vulnerable communities. SS *Hope* was retired from service in 1974, yet Project HOPE's land-based medical activities are still inspired by the ship's initial mission. The charity has trained over two million medical professionals and has donated over $2 billion dollars' worth of medication and supplies.

projecthope.org

Find hope in the 2020 Refugee Olympic Team

The Refugee Olympic Team was created ahead of the 2016 Olympics in Rio de Janeiro. Comprising athletes who have been forced to flee their home countries, the Refugee Olympic Team sends a clear message of hope to the millions of refugees who have been displaced as a result of war or natural disaster. When announcing the new team, Thomas Bach, the International Olympic Committee President, called for compassion, mutual respect and recognition of the contributions of refugees.

At the 2020 games, held in Tokyo in 2021, 29 athletes from the Refugee Olympic Team competed across 12 sports. Athletes included Syrian refugee Sanda Aldass (judo) and Rose Nathike Lokonyen (athletics), who fled South Sudan. All were hailed for their courage.

olympics.com/ioc/refugee-olympic-team

Inspire hope in other people

Help

Offer support

Praise

Encourage

Remember that hopes and dreams, like butterflies, soar when they are set free.

Hope = justified expectation.

French philosopher René Descartes tackled the idea of hope in his 1649 work *Passions of the Soul*. He recognized hope as one of the 'Passions of the Soul', and the foundation upon which boldness and courage are built.

The 18th-century German philosopher Immanuel Kant defined hope as the 'unexpected offering of the prospect of immeasurable good fortune'.

Søren Kierkegaard believed that hope is both an eternal and a possible expectation for good.

" *Therefore, never unlovingly give up on any human being or give up hope for that person, since it is possible that even the most prodigal son could still be saved, that even the most embittered enemy - alas, he who was your friend - it is still possible that he could again become your friend. It is possible that the one who sank the deepest - alas, because he stood so high - it is still possible that he could again be raised up. It is still possible that the love that became cold could again begin to burn.* "

SØREN KIERKEGAARD

"Hope is a passion for the possible."

SØREN KIERKEGAARD

While Friedrich Nietzsche is often remembered for his critical and negative beliefs, even he could not help but place hope among the 'strong emotions'.

"Hope is the rainbow over the cascading stream of life."

FRIEDRICH NIETZSCHE

"That mankind be redeemed from revenge: that to me is the bridge to the highest hope and a rainbow after long thunderstorms."

FRIEDRICH NIETZSCHE

"After despair, there's still hope, so be wise:
After the darkness, many suns will rise."

RUMI

The old cliché proclaims that 'it is always darkest before the dawn'. This can help to remind us that, even when things seem bleakest, a new beginning – and a ray of hope – can be much closer than we appreciate.

Remember the darkness before dawn

In your mind, carefully return to a dark moment when all hope seemed to be lost: when you suffered a broken heart; when there was a family falling-out; when someone close to you was injured. Recall your feelings at that time. Then, try to recall the moment when you found that flicker of hope that kept you going. Perhaps you didn't find it immediately, and perhaps your hope came from an unexpected source – but it is worth remembering that better times always return.

By remembering that dawn follows the darkness, you help to condition your mind into remembering that hope is not only valid, but essential to life.

"Hope is the only bee that makes honey without flowers."

ROBERT GREEN INGERSOLL

Don't be deceived by the airy
nature of hope. 'I hope for this',
'I hope for that'...

The very act of hoping is dynamic.
Hope is an action that helps you
visualize and achieve your goal.

Begin a hope success log

If hoping seems hopeless, begin a hope success log to remind yourself of when your hopes have come true. Recall every flicker of hope you can, from small hopes, such as 'I hope my son passes his spelling test', to big hopes, such as 'I hope my friend's surgery is successful'. By looking back on moments when hopes became reality, you will find the strength to keep on hoping.

Hope is. . .

Your invisible friend.

Your comforter.

Your cheerleader.

Your path through difficult times.

Journal your way to a more hopeful outlook

However you order your day, whether it's in to-do lists, diaries or gratitude journals, introduce the concept of hope to your journaling. Set a daily intention to remain hopeful or follow one of these hopeful journal prompts. When planning ahead, keep hope at the front of your mind.

Hopeful journal prompts

I feel hopeful today because. . .

Today I shared my hopes with. . .

When viewed with hope, this situation feels. . .

I will allow hope to flourish by. . .

I feel sad, but I will hold on to hope by. . .

"O sweet To-morrow!—
After to-day
There will away
This sense of sorrow.
Then let us borrow
Hope, for a gleaming
Soon will be streaming,
Dimmed by no gray—
No gray!

While the winds wing us
Sighs from The Gone,
Nearer to dawn
Minute-beats bring us;
When there will sing us
Larks of a glory

Waiting our story
Further anon—
Anon!

Doff the black token,
Don the red shoon,
Right and retune
Viol-strings broken;
Null the words spoken
In speeches of rueing,
The night cloud is hueing,
To-morrow shines soon—
Shines soon!"

THOMAS HARDY
'Song of Hope'

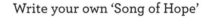

Write your own 'Song of Hope'

Hopes need to be tangible. Ask yourself questions about your hopes, expectations and dreams. Write down what you desire, no matter how outlandish, and begin to build pathways to each of your hopeful destinations.

'Song of Hope' prompts

Today, I hope. . .

Tomorrow, I hope. . .

This week, I hope. . .

This month, I hope. . .

This year, I hope. . .

For my physical self, I hope. . .

For my emotional self, I hope. . .

For my spiritual self, I hope. . .

For my romantic self, I hope. . .

For my lover, I hope…

For my parents, I hope…

For my children, I hope…

For my friends, I hope…

For my community, I hope…

For my country, I hope…

For my planet, I hope…

To hope is to express confidence in yourself, in life, in the future. To hope is a bold expression that good will follow bad, that light will follow darkness and that life's journey is to be embraced.

Have the confidence to proceed, full of hope and with merriness in your heart.

Hope is a two-stage process:

1. Hope comforts you now. Hope makes present hardships easier to bear.

2. Hope shows you a vision of a better future. Hope illuminates your journey onwards.

"Hope is the most universal of human possessions."

THALES OF MILETUS

"'Hope' is the thing with feathers –
That perches in the soul –
And sings the tune without the words –
And never stops – at all –

And sweetest – in the Gale – is heard –
And sore must be the storm –
That could abash the little Bird
That kept so many warm –

I've heard it in the chillest land –
And on the strangest Sea –
Yet – never – in Extremity,
It asked a crumb – of me."

EMILY DICKINSON

Emily Dickinson was a reclusive American poet from 19th-century Massachusetts. She dressed in white, loved to bake and wrote over 1,800 poems. Her words are fragile, tender, light and piercingly astute.

Her most famous poem, 'Hope is the thing with feathers', sees Dickinson imagining hope as a bird that sings and flies through storms and extremities. Her final line, that hope never 'asked a crumb – of me' suggests that hoping costs us nothing. It is a marvellous image: our soul's hope still singing amidst calamity.

Create your own 'thing with feathers'

1. Visualize your own personal emblem of hope.

2. Sketch or find an image of your 'thing with feathers' – is it a delicate song thrush, majestic swan or mythical phoenix?

3. Close your eyes and feel how it 'perches in the soul'.

4. When you find yourself in the 'chillest land' or 'strangest sea', reach for your fluttering 'thing with feathers' and feel your hope singing still.

Hope is saying. . .

"It'll be OK."

"I'm here for you."

"We'll get through this."

"You are not alone."

Hope is present. . .

in the kindness of strangers.

in the innocence of children.

in the dedication of teachers.

in a baby's smile.

in the wise eyes of your grandparents.

in the mirror every morning.

" There is neither happiness nor unhappiness in this world; there is only the comparison of one state with another. Only a man who has felt ultimate despair is capable of feeling ultimate bliss. It is necessary to have wished for death in order to know how good it is to live... the sum of all human wisdom will be contained in these two words: Wait and Hope."

ALEXANDRE DUMAS
The Count of Monte Cristo

Lofn is the Norse goddess of forbidden love. Mild and loving, Lofn is a gentle goddess who has the power to unite couples whose love is frowned upon in society or by family. She provides hope that love can triumph over attitudes and beliefs.

Hang up fairy lights and feel the glow

Give the harsh lighting a miss and bring a little warmth to your living space. The comforting glow will help remind you that even when darkness is present, hope is not lost.

"The essence of optimism is not its view of the present, but the fact that it is the inspiration of life and hope when others give in; it enables a man to hold his head high when everything seems to be going wrong; it gives him strength to sustain reverses and yet to claim the future for himself instead of abandoning it to his opponent."

DIETRICH BONHOEFFER

What distinguishes hope from daydreaming is our capacity to act on our hopes.

Hope + action = success.

"Is there another world for this frail dust
To warm with life and be itself again?
Something about me daily speaks there must,
And why should instinct nourish hopes in vain?
'Tis nature's prophesy that such will be,
And everything seems struggling to explain
The close sealed volume of its mystery.
Time wandering onward keeps its usual pace
As seeming anxious of eternity,
To meet that calm and find a resting place.

E'en the small violet feels a future power
And waits each year renewing blooms to bring,
And surely man is no inferior flower
To die unworthy of a second spring?"

JOHN CLARE
'The Instinct of Hope'

Hope says. . .

"Keep going."

"Don't give up."

"Try, try and try again."

"Persist."

"It gets easier."

"Delve within; within is the fountain of good, and it is always ready to bubble up, if you always delve."

MARCUS AURELIUS

Hope is contagious.

Hope starts with a small flame and burns ever brighter.

Hope spreads among open hearts.

Some of the most poignant symbols of hope can be found in the bleakest of settings. Out of the trenches of World War I, where soldiers' bodies lay, grew flame-red poppies. The profusion of poppies amidst the carnage in the spring of 1915 caught the eye of one Canadian soldier, John McCrae. His famed poem 'In Flanders Fields' helped the red poppy become the lasting memorial symbol to the fallen, showing that even from death and tragedy, there is the potential for not just life, but beauty.

"In Flanders fields the poppies blow
Between the crosses, row on row,
*   That mark our place; and in the sky*
*   The larks, still bravely singing, fly*
Scarce heard amid the guns below.

We are the Dead. Short days ago
We lived, felt dawn, saw sunset glow,
*   Loved and were loved, and now we lie,*
*   In Flanders fields.*

Take up our quarrel with the foe:
To you from failing hands we throw
*   The torch; be yours to hold it high.*
*   If ye break faith with us who die*
We shall not sleep, though poppies
grow
*   In Flanders fields.*"

JOHN MCCRAE
'In Flanders Fields'

Ground Zero is a manifestation of hope triumphing over darkness. The site of the Twin Towers terrorist atrocity of September 11, 2001, is now one of the most moving museums in the world. It is a testament to the power of love and survival over death and destruction. Celebrating the bravery of the first responders and rescuers, the love in people's last messages, and the sheer will of New Yorkers to rise together, stronger, from the rubble, Ground Zero is a commemoration of hope in times of adversity.

The official blog of the 9/11 Memorial and Museum features 'stories of hope', which offer a positive and hopeful response to one of America's darkest days.

911memorial.org

To hold hope in your heart is not to deny difficulties but to look forwards, to visualize what life might look like on the other side. Being hopeful helps us to work through our present problems. The more we hope, the bigger our capacity for hopefulness.

Written when the Romantic poet Keats was only 19, 'To Hope' illustrates the young poet as he fends off melancholy, despair and other such evils with the gentle assistance of hope. He ends each verse by entreating hope to wave 'thy silver pinions o'er my head!'.

" *When by my solitary hearth I sit,*
And hateful thoughts enwrap my soul
in gloom;
When no fair dreams before my 'mind's
eye' flit,
And the bare heath of life presents no
bloom;
Sweet Hope, ethereal balm upon me
shed,
And wave thy silver pinions o'er my
head!

Whene'er I wander, at the fall of night,
Where woven boughs shut out the
moon's bright ray,

Should sad Despondency my musings fright,
And frown, to drive fair Cheerfulness away,
Peep with the moon-beams through the leafy roof,
And keep that fiend Despondence far aloof!

Should Disappointment, parent of Despair,
Strive for her son to seize my careless heart;
When, like a cloud, he sits upon the air,
Preparing on his spell-bound prey to dart:

Chase him away, sweet Hope, with visage bright,
And fright him as the morning frightens night!

Whene'er the fate of those I hold most dear
Tells to my fearful breast a tale of sorrow,
O bright-eyed Hope, my morbid fancy cheer;
Let me awhile thy sweetest comforts borrow:
Thy heaven-born radiance around me shed,
And wave thy silver pinions o'er my head!

Should e'er unhappy love my bosom
pain,
From cruel parents, or relentless fair;
O let me think it is not quite in vain
To sigh out sonnets to the midnight air!
Sweet Hope, ethereal balm upon me
shed,
And wave thy silver pinions o'er my
head!

In the long vista of the years to roll,
Let me not see our country's honour
fade:
O let me see our land retain her soul,
Her pride, her freedom; and not
freedom's shade.

From thy bright eyes unusual
brightness shed –
Beneath thy pinions canopy my head!

Let me not see the patriot's high
bequest,
Great Liberty! how great in plain attire!
With the base purple of a court
oppress'd,
Bowing her head, and ready to expire:
But let me see thee stoop from heaven
on wings
That fill the skies with silver glitterings!

And as, in sparkling majesty, a star
Gilds the bright summit of some
gloomy cloud;
Brightening the half veil'd face of
heaven afar:
So, when dark thoughts my boding
spirit shroud,
Sweet Hope, celestial influence round
me shed,
Waving thy silver pinions o'er my
head!"

JOHN KEATS
'To Hope'

Make silver pinions to wave o'er thy head

Pinions are the outer part of a bird's feathers – including the flight feathers. Create your own hopeful talisman by assembling a beautiful selection of feathers and hanging them where you would most like them to 'wave o'er thy head'.

" The man who does not believe in miracles surely makes it certain that he will never take part in one."

WILLIAM BLAKE

When problem-solving, frame questions in a way that incorporates hopefulness

How hopeful am I that this can be resolved?

What outcome am I hoping for?

Can we hope that this solution will last?

Borrow someone else's hope

When times are so upsetting that you feel there is no hope, borrow someone else's. Ask yourself: what makes my mum optimistic for the future? What does my cheerful colleague do to stay strong in dark times? Explore other people's self-care rituals for remaining hopeful. If a close friend gets a dose of positivity from daily walks in nature, or your brother finds hope by volunteering at the local community centre, borrow their methods of remaining optimistic until you are able to rediscover your own hope. It will return.

Share in the hope of the rescued Chilean miners

When a copper-gold mine collapsed in Copiapó, Chile, the world focused its hopes on the fate of the 33 miners, who were trapped 700 metres underground and five kilometres from the mine's entrance. Their miraculous rescue was an astonishing act of human endeavour, hope and bravery, which captured the hearts of even the most cynical. Above ground, the Chilean government, NASA, the Vatican and 12 corporations all co-operated on the mechanics of the rescue bid. From the Pope sending rosaries, to the design of special rescue pods by the Chilean Navy and NASA, the international collaboration to sustain and rescue the miners was immense. Below ground, the 33 miners had to work together to keep hope alive and morale high. The miners assumed different roles; a doctor, a religious leader, a humourist. They formed a 'one man, one vote' democracy, deciding on coping strategies and practical issues as a group.

The 33 were eventually rescued 69 days after the collapse – proving that incredible feats can be achieved when the flame of hope burns brightly.

"There is no medicine like hope, no incentive so great, and no tonic so powerful as expectation of something tomorrow."

ORISON SWETT MARDEN

"The phoenix hope, can wing her flight
Thro' the vast deserts of the skies,
And still defying fortune's spite;
Revive, and from her ashes rise."

MIGUEL DE CERVANTES SAAVEDRA

"*My dear friend*
Never lose hope
when the beloved
sends you away.

If you're abandoned
if you're left hopeless
tomorrow for sure
you'll be called again.

If the door is shut
right in your face
keep waiting with patience
don't leave right away.

Seeing your patience
your love will soon
summon you with grace
raise you like a champion.

And if all the roads
End up in dead ends
You'll be shown the secret paths
No one will comprehend."

RUMI

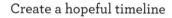

Create a hopeful timeline

If the weight of the world is heavy upon your heart, anchor yourself in the progress that has already been made. Remind yourself of the achievements of others against all the odds. Draw sustenance from acts of hope from history. Remember that, up until the very moment that these things happened, they were not guaranteed. They were willed into existence on the waves of hope.

Past events that inspire hope for the future

1928 All women gain the right to vote in the UK.

1942 Discovery of penicillin.

1963 Martin Luther King's 'I Have a Dream' speech.

1978 Birth of Louise Brown, the first IVF baby.

1989 Demolition of Berlin Wall.

1990 Nelson Mandela released from prison.

Barack Obama's second book, *The Audacity of Hope*, written while he was still a Senator, sought to reclaim the American dream. Published in 2006, it sold millions of copies worldwide and secured Obama's reputation as the embodiment of hopeful and optimistic politics.

Hope was a theme in many of Obama's speeches, including his famous 2008 Iowa Caucus Speech.

Be inspired by the hope of Tim Berners-Lee

Can one man really have invented the internet? Sure. Step forward computer scientist Professor Sir Tim Berners-Lee, who invented the World Wide Web in 1989. Rather than charging every user 1p, he decided that the web ought to be free for all. While he was responsible for one of the greatest intellectual advances in human history, Tim Berners-Lee's aspirations for the internet were straightforward – he wanted to create connection.

Choose hope.

Choose optimism.

Choose positivity.

Choose progress.

Choose hope, always.

Baby names to inspire hope

Aurora: Latin name meaning 'sunshine', 'new break of day'

Asha: Hindi name meaning 'hope', 'life'

Dawn: a new day, a new life

Hope: desire of fulfilment

Nadine: French name meaning 'hope'

Nina: Hebrew name meaning 'grace of God'

Vita: Latin for 'life'

Lakshmi, the Hindu goddess whose name means 'she who leads to one's goal', is the wife of the god Vishnu. Lakshmi is depicted with four arms, representing the four tenets of Hinduism: *dharm* (pursuit of an ethical life), *artha* (pursuit of prosperity), *kama*, (pursuit of emotional fulfilment) and *moksha* (pursuit of self-knowledge). In Sanskrit, Lakshmi means to 'know and understand one's goal.' This powerful goddess thus embodies ideas of hope, forward momentum and purpose through life.

"When you get into a tight place, and everything goes against you, till it seems as if you couldn't hold on a minute longer, never give up then, for that's just the place and time that the tide'll turn."

HARRIET BEECHER STOWE

Hope is. . .

A decision.

An act of bravery.

A choice.

"Verily, with every difficulty there is relief."

QURAN 94:5-6

"Hope is patience with the lamp lit."

TERTULLIAN

Draw hope from the knowledge that the heart has an infinite capacity to love.

"*Oh, Hope! thou soother sweet of human woes!*

How shall I lure thee to my haunts forlorn!
For me wilt thou renew the withered rose,

And clear my painful path of pointed thorn?
Ah come, sweet nymph! in smiles and softness drest,

Like the young hours that lead the tender year
Enchantress come! and charm my cares to rest:

Alas! the flatterer flies, and will not hear!

A prey to fear, anxiety, and pain,
    Must I a sad existence still deplore?
Lo! the flowers fade, but all the thorns
remain,
    'For me the vernal garland blooms
no more.'
Come then, 'pale Misery's love!' be thou
my cure,
And I will bless thee, who tho' slow,
art sure.**"**

CHARLOTTE SMITH

Project Hope Exchange is an initiative to build a huge online collection of messages of hope borne out of adversity and suffering. Each message is a 30-second audio clip communicating hope – so that we can share in each other's experiences and strengths, and avoid feelings of hopelessness.

The messages of hope are divided into three categories of adversity: physical health, mental health and life's challenges. Search for a message on a struggle similar to your own and when you press play, you will hear a human voice reach out across the internet. Each message reminds us that we are not alone, and that we can be strong still. There is hope, and there are other people like us.

It's a wonderful initiative and leaves visitors to the website with hope aflame in their hearts once more.

projecthopeexchange.com

Think of hope as an ember that burns gently in your heart. It can be revived with...

Enthusiasm

Positivity

Endeavour

Enquiry

Curiosity

Optimism

Courage

Three simple ways to reignite hope

1. Read powerful stories of hope triumphing over adversity.

2. Spend time with optimistic and resilient friends.

3. Re-focus on your objectives, and check in with yourself regularly.

Two powerful stories of hope triumphing over adversity

Selwa Hussain was the first woman in the UK to live without a human heart. After suffering from heart failure in 2017, Selwa was given a fully artificial heart that she carried around with her in a rucksack for 16 months. She received a human heart transplant in 2018 and now lives a full, happy life. She and her team of doctors embody the hope that modern medicine brings.

Erik Weihenmayer lost his sight at the age of 13, but that didn't stop him from climbing Mount Everest in 2001. He went on to climb all of the Seven Summits – the highest peaks on all seven continents. Determined not to let his sight-loss destroy his enjoyment of life, Erik founded No Barriers, a charity to help people tap into their inner hope, optimism and resilience.

nobarriersusa.org

Inspired by Captain Tom, the British nonagenarian who walked around his garden raising money for the NHS during the 2020 lockdown, Anne and Joel Buckland created the podcast *100 Stories of Hope*. The couple marked what would have been Captain Tom's 101st birthday with encouragement and messages to inspire. With voices from charities, faith groups and individuals with hopeful insights to share, the podcast offers 100 short, blazing blasts of hope.

anchor.fm/100-stories-of-hope

*"Hope is a lover's staff; walk hence with that
And manage it against despairing thoughts."*

WILLIAM SHAKESPEARE
Two Gentlemen of Verona

Trying to get a novel published?

Don't give up hope!

- Multimillion best-selling author J.K. Rowling received rejections from 12 different publishers for *Harry Potter and the Philosopher's Stone* before Bloomsbury saw the magic in her writing.

- When Audrey Niffenegger's *The Time Traveller's Wife* was rejected 25 times by agents, she sent it directly to small San Francisco publisher MacAdam/Cage. It went on to sell 2.5 million copies and was later turned into a blockbuster Hollywood film.

- Stephen King's *Carrie* was rejected 30 times by publishers before Doubleday snapped it up and launched the career of the world's leading horror writer.

While Abraham Lincoln is now remembered as one of history's finest men and the president who ended slavery, his earlier political life was beset with failure.

If he had lost hope then, how different would world history have been?

Lincoln's bumpy road to success – remember this and DON'T LOSE HOPE!

Defeated when running for state legislature in 1832.

Failed in business in 1833.

Elected to state legislature in 1834.

Sweetheart died in 1835.

Had a nervous breakdown in 1836.

Defeated when running for Speaker in 1838.

Defeated when running for Congress in 1843.

Elected to Congress in 1846.

Lost renomination in 1848.

Rejected when running for land officer in 1849.

Defeated when running for U.S. Senate in 1854.

Defeated when running for Vice President in 1856.

Again defeated when running for U.S. Senate in 1858.

Elected President in 1860.

"Clouds and darkness surround us, yet Heaven is just, and the day of triumph will surely come, when justice and truth will be vindicated."

MARY TODD LINCOLN

Hope can be found in. . .

The sun rising every morning.

Nature reawakening every spring.

A warm cup of tea.

"Oh Wind,
If winter comes, can spring be
far behind?"

PERCY BYSSHE SHELLEY

Hope needs a vast landscape. Try not to pin it down too firmly; give it space to breathe and fly before you. It will take you to vistas you have never before dreamed of.

Tips for trying not to pin your hopes too firmly

1. Avoid pinning hopes on outside sources. When you have established what you are hoping for, ask yourself whether you can do anything to bring it closer to reality. For example, if you hope to be able to afford a deposit for a flat, make sure you've established a savings plan and are not merely banking on winning the lottery.

2. Be careful to avoid freighting someone else with all of your hopes and dreams. Pinning all your hopes on one person is a big responsibility for them. Keep

personal hopes as broad as possible to avoid crashing heartache if that person cannot deliver.

3. Be conscious of the pain of clinging on to specific dates and places. Does the holiday absolutely have to take place on that date and at that specific hotel? By practising flexibility, it is more likely that broader hopes and dreams will be met.

"It seems to me we can never give up longing and wishing while we are thoroughly alive. There are certain things we feel to be beautiful and good, and we must hunger after them."

GEORGE ELIOT

"Hope is like a harebell trembling from its birth,
Love is like a rose, the joy of all the earth;
Faith is like a lily lifted high and white,
Love is like a lovely rose, the world's delight;
Harebells and sweet lilies show a thornless growth,
But the rose with all its thorns excels them both."

CHRISTINA ROSSETTI

Through the frozen earth, a slender green shoot prises itself upwards. Soon, on a stone-cold January day, the snowdrop will open its teardrop petals and *galanthus nivalis* will herald the start of spring.

Plant snowdrop bulbs as the ultimate representation of new starts

When cold weather comes, you will be reminded that new life is eternal and that even in the darkest days of winter, there is hope.

Spring is the time to bathe yourself in hope. As the sun warms and the sap rises, the miracle of nature once again tenderly emerges from the cold grip of winter. Tune in to the world around you, immerse yourself in the hope that new lambs bring, let the warmth of the sun fill your heart with optimism, and remind yourself that new hopes and new life are possible, no matter how barren and frozen the ground appears.

How to make the most of the hope that spring brings

1. Hike. Bike. Walk in nature.

2. Open the windows.

3. Turn your face to the sun.

4. Make the most of increased daylight to boost vitamin D.

5. Fill vases with daffodils.

"*When the mind has a tendency to dream, it is a mistake to keep dreams away from it, to ration its dreams. So long as you distract your mind from its dreams, it will not know them for what they are; you will always be being taken in by the appearance of things, because you will not have grasped their true nature. If a little dreaming is dangerous, the cure for it is not to dream less but to dream more, to dream all the time.*"

MARCEL PROUST

" Though the breath of disappointment should chill the sanguine heart, speedily it gloweth again, warmed by the live embers of hope."

MARTIN F. TUPPER

Rick Snyder, the pioneering American positive psychologist, defined hope as a cognitive trait that helps people to recognize and pursue their goals. He identified two components of hope that distinguish it from mere wishful thinking.

1. Pathways: the capacity to visualize the strategies necessary to achieve your goals.

2. Agency: the ability and motivation to follow those pathways.

"All Nature seems at work. Slugs leave their lair –
The bees are stirring – birds are on the wing –
And Winter slumbering in the open air,
Wears on his smiling face a dream of Spring!
And I the while, the sole unbusy thing,
Nor honey make, nor pair, nor build, nor sing.

Yet well I ken the banks where amaranths blow,
Have traced the fount whence streams of nectar flow.

Bloom, O ye amaranths! bloom for whom ye may,
For me ye bloom not! Glide, rich streams, away!
With lips unbrightened, wreathless brow, I stroll:
And would you learn the spells that drowse my soul?
Work without Hope draws nectar in a sieve,
And Hope without an object cannot live."

SAMUEL TAYLOR COLERIDGE
'Work without Hope'

Samuel Taylor Coleridge, that most dashing Romantic poet, imagines himself lounging around watching the busy bees of nature and waiting for artistic inspiration. The final two lines of his poem 'Work without Hope' read: 'Work without Hope draws nectar in a sieve, / And Hope without an object cannot live.' In his languid way, he reminds us that working without anything to strive for is unlikely to bring useful results; equally, hoping in a vague sense is pointless – you must have an object or goal to focus on.

Do what you can to spread ripples of hope: be kind, be generous, forgive, smile. Ripples of hope will spread about you.

To increase your capacity for hope, make sure you practise consistent self-care

Factor in regular relaxation, stimulation and connection. It's also important to factor in the more difficult parts of self-care: get regular check-ups at the doctor, get up and outside even when you don't feel like it, clean the pile of washing-up that's been hanging around for days. It's easier to feel hopeful when you take life step-by-step.

Join America in celebrating April as the National Month of Hope

Following calls from the charity Mothers in Crisis, April was first designated as the National Month of Hope in 2018. The slogan for the first month of hope was 'I would rather hope'.

Five ways to celebrate the National Month of Hope in April

1. Volunteer to help children read at your local school.

2. Form a meaningful connection with someone you don't yet know in your neighbourhood.

3. Give your time to someone who appreciates it.

4. Tidy up your immediate surroundings.

5. Smile at all you see.

Helping

Others

Practise

Empowerment

Helping others when they've lost hope can be one of the greatest acts of service you can perform. Hope can slip away when people think they are not worthy of happiness. By sharing your hope, it will expand to fill their emptiness.

1. Remind them that they are loved and worthy of happiness.

2. Recognize their predicament and show concern.

3. Extend the hand of kindness.

4. Help them look beyond their weaknesses and flaws.

5. Encourage them to seek professional help, if needed.

6. Keeping checking in.

7. Celebrate together as hope returns.

Think of hope as a friend holding your hand in your darkest hour.

Discover the connection between hope and creativity

In a study published in the *Journal of Business Research,* Portuguese scientists studied 203 employees and discovered a link between their individual creativity and how hopeful they felt. When faced with a problem, those who are able to offer a variety of creative solutions feel more hopeful.

Meet 'waypower', hope's secret weapon

'Waypower' has been identified as a mental capacity we can call on to find one or more effective ways to reach our goals. Where willpower might be the engine, waypower is the Sat Nav directing our activities towards hopeful outcomes.

Create a waypower hope map

Write your hope along the top of your map. Then, like the roots of a tree, create different waypower pathways to reach your goal. Some may lead nowhere and others may branch off in different directions, but one will certainly meet with hope.

We all remember the magical thrill of throwing a penny into a fountain and making a wish. There was always a faint whisper of hope that it might come true. Wishing wells and the like are not mere superstitious follies, but rather respond to the innate human desire to hope for a certain outcome.

The modern-day equivalent of a wishing well is a 'hope map'. Developed by Dr Shane Lopez, the hope map is a straightforward way to visualize your dreams and begin the realistic road to making them happen. First, it's worth identifying barriers to hope that might come up along the way.

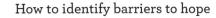

How to identify barriers to hope

1. Find your favourite notebook. And a pen. And a lovely big bar of chocolate. Take yourself to somewhere beautiful where you won't be interrupted.

2. Ask yourself: What is preventing you from feeling hopeful? Is it fear of failure? Fear of beginning? Anxiety about what's involved?

3. Jot down all the barriers to hope that easily come to mind. Include any barriers that seem a little silly or embarrassing.

4. Drill down. For each of the barriers, get specific. What aspect of failure do you find particularly daunting, for example?

5. By visualizing the barriers to hope, you may begin to see that they are not as strong as you first imagined. In fact, the barriers may be rather flimsy, and you may find that with an optimistic attitude, you'll be able to knock them aside without too much effort. Now you can use them to create a hope map and strategize your path to success.

Create a hope map

1. Place a piece of paper horizontally on your desk. Divide it vertically into thirds. Label the first section 'Tactics', the middle section 'Barriers' and, finally, the third section 'Hopes'.

2. If you are artistically inclined, sketch a rainbow or other symbol of hope over the three sections.

3. Identify your goals and write them in the 'Hopes' section. Then, work backwards through 'Barriers' and then to 'Tactics'. Think carefully about what is necessary to make your hopes a reality.

If you want to increase your hope quota, spend time with someone hopeful

Not only will their enthusiasm rub off on you, but you'll also be on your way to creating a support network – an essential for when life seems glum.

Hope rises from. . .

Shattered dreams.

Broken hearts.

Grieving souls.

Hope, as your phoenix, rises
from the ashes of adversity and
flies from darkness to light.

Find hope in the Natural History Museum

Swinging from the cavernous ceiling of London's Natural History Museum is Hope, the skeleton of a 25.2 metre blue whale. Relocated in 2017 from the Mammals gallery to Hintze Hall, the blue whale skeleton now greets tourists and visitors as they enter the Museum.

The whale was named Hope to reflect that it is still within our power to create a sustainable future for the planet. Hope represents the fortunes of blue whales, whose numbers have risen from a low of 400 in 1966 to around 20,000 today, following the ban on commercial whaling in the 1980s. If the fortunes of the blue whale can be so improved by human effort, there is hope for the rest of the planet.

In February 2021, the United Arab Emirates space probe *Misbar Al-Amal* (Hope) entered the orbit of Mars after its launch in July 2020. The name Hope was chosen from 1,000 submitted entries, and was selected to send a message of optimism across the globe.

Learn three hope-filled words:

Meliorism: the belief that the world can be made better by human effort.

Apricity: the warmth of the sun on a cold winter's day.

Respair: a recovery, a return to hope.

How to say 'hope' around the world

Albania: *shpresoj*

Bosnia: *nada*

Denmark: *håber*

Estonia: *lootus*

Finland: *toivoa*

Germany: *Hoffnung*

Hungary: *remény*

Italy: *speranza*

Japan: *nozomu*

Lithuania: *viltis*

Malta: *tama*

Norway: *håp*

Poland: *nadzieja*

Spain: *esperanza*

Turkey: *umut*

Ukraine: *nadiyus'*

Wales: *gobaith*

Hope doesn't. . .

Quit.

Turn back.

Give up.

Hope...

Endures.

Nourishes.

Strengthens.

Create a hopeful self-care ritual

We all face moments of hopelessness. That's where hopeful self-care comes in. Decide on a movie with a hopeful message, pick out your favourite mug and a warming drink, get cosy with a candle or some fairy lights and let your hope be reignited.

Remember first and foremost to be gentle with yourself. It's OK to feel fragile in difficult moments, and it's OK to ask for professional help if you're still struggling to reignite your spark.

We all have fears and doubts, yet there are always things to hope for, if we only dare to dream.

" How wonderful it is that nobody need wait a single moment before starting to improve the world. "

ANNE FRANK

MAKE HOPE HAPPEN

QUOTES ARE TAKEN FROM

Alexandre Dumas, 1802–1870 French author

Alexander Pope, 1688–1744, English poet

Alfred, Lord Tennyson, 1809–1892, British poet

Charlotte Smith, 1749–1806, English poet and novelist

Christina Rossetti, 1830–1894, English poet

Dietrich Bonhoeffer, 1906–1945, German theologian

Diogenes, c. 412–323 BC, Ancient Greek philosopher who lived in a barrel

Emily Dickinson, 1830–1886, American poet and recluse

Franklin D. Roosevelt, 1882–1945, 32nd American President

Friedrich Nietzsche, 1844–1900, 19th-century German philosopher and cultural critic

George Eliot, 1819–1880, English author – real name Mary Anne Evans

Harriet Beecher Stowe, 1811–1896, American abolitionist and writer

Immanuel Kant, 1724–1804, German philosopher

John Keats, 1795–1821, English Romantic poet

John McCrae, 1872–1918, Canadian war poet

Marcus Aurelius, 121–180 AD, Roman Emperor and philosopher

Marcel Proust, 1871–1922, French author and enjoyer of madeleines

Martin F. Tupper, 1810–1889, English philosopher

Mary Todd Lincoln, 1818–1882, First Lady of the United States 1861–1865

Miguel de Cervantes Saavedra, 1547–1616, Spanish writer of *Don Quixote*

Orison Swett Marden, 1848–1924, American author

Percy Bysshe Shelley, 1792–1822, English Romantic poet

René Descartes, 1596–1650, French philosopher and mathematician

Robert Green Ingersoll, 1833–1899, American writer and orator

Rumi, 1207–1273, Persian poet

Samuel Taylor Coleridge, 1772–1834, English Romantic poet

Socrates, c. 470–c. 399 BC, Greek philosopher

Søren Aabye Kierkegaard, 1813–1855, Danish philosopher

Thales of Miletus, c. 626–623—c. 548–545 BC, pre-Socratic philosopher

Thomas Hardy, 1840–1928, English author

Tertullian , 155–220 AD, early Christian author

William Blake 1757–1827 English poet

William Shakespeare, 1564–1616 English playwright extraordinaire

HOPEFUL READING LIST

Making Hope Happen, Shane J. Lopez, Atria Books, 2014

Psychology of Hope, C. R. Snyder, Simon & Schuster, 2000

Handbook of Hope, C. R. Snyder, Academic Press, 2000

Hope in the Age of Anxiety, Anthony Scioli and Henry Biller, OUP, 2009

Oxford Dictionary of Quotations, ed. Elizabeth Knowles, 8th ed., OUP, 2009

The New Penguin Book of Romantic Poetry, ed. by Jonathan and Jessica Wordsworth, Penguin Classics, 2005

The Oxford Book of English Verse, ed. by Christopher Ricks, OUP, 1999

HOPEFUL WEBSITES

psychologytoday.com

ideas.ted.com/how-to-be-more-hopeful/

humanprogress.org

ourworldindata.org

SCHOLARLY ARTICLES CITED

Rego, A., Machado, F., Leal, S., & Cunha, M.P.E. (2009), 'Are hopeful employees more creative? An empirical study', *Creativity Research Journal* 21 (2-3) 223-231. DOI: 10.1080/10400410902858733

Snyder, C. R. (2002), 'Hope theory: rainbows in the mind', *Psychological Inquiry* 13(4), 249-275. DOI: 10.1207/S15327965PLI1304_01

Snyder, C. R., Harris, C., Anderson, J. R., Holleran, S. A., Irving, L. M., Sigmon, S. T., *et al* (1991), 'The will and the ways: development and validation of an individual-differences measure of hope', *J. Pers. Soc. Psychol.* 60 (4), 570-585. DOI: 10.1037/0022-3514.60.4.570

Snyder, C. R., Hoza, B., Pelham, W. E., Rapoff, M., Ware, L., Danovsky, M., *et al* (1997), 'The development and validation of the children's hope scale', *J. Pediatr. Psychol.* 22 (3), 399-421. DOI: 10.1093/jpepsy/22.3.399

Mohammadi S. D., Moslemi Z., Ghomi M. (2019), 'The Relationship between Hope Components with Academic Burnout, Motivation, and Status of Students in Qom University of Medical Sciences, Qom, Iran', *Journal of Medical Education Development* 12 (35), 27–36.

Rego. A., Sousa, F., Marques, C., Cunha, M.P.E. (2014) 'Hope and positive affect mediating the authentic leadership and creativity relationship', *Journal of Business Research,* 67 (2), 200–210.

Publishing Director Sarah Lavelle
Editorial Assistant Sofie Shearman
Words Joanna Gray
Series Designer Emily Lapworth
Designer Alicia House
Head of Production Stephen Lang
Production Controller Sabeena Atchia

Published in 2022 by Quadrille,
an imprint of Hardie Grant
Publishing

Quadrille
52–54 Southwark Street
London SE1 1UN
quadrille.com

The publisher has made every
effort to trace the copyright
holders. We apologize in advance
for any unintentional omissions
and would be pleased to insert the
appropriate acknowledgement in
any subsequent edition.

Cataloguing in Publication Data:
a catalogue record for this book is
available from the British Library.

ISBN 978 1 78713 803 2

Printed in China